Presented to

MR. P. A. DICK

in gratitude for his service

as a Trustee on the

BOARD OF THE SOUTHWESTERN
REGIONAL LIBRARY SYSTEM

November 28, 1979

H. Ford, Secretary-Treasurer

ACKNOWLEDGED.
PAID DEC - 8 1979

Seasons of Canada

Author: Val Clery

Photographer: Bill Brooks

Designer: René Demers
Craib Demers Associates Limited

Publisher: Anthony Hawke

Printer: Heritage Press

Typesetting: Kerr Graphics Limited

Copyright© 1979 by
Val Clery and Bill Brooks
All rights reserved
ISBN 0-88882-041-0

The song, from which lines are
quoted in the text, is "Mon Pays",
written by Gilles Vigneault.

Hounslow Press
A Division of Anthony R. Hawke Limited
124 Parkview Avenue
Willowdale, Ontario, Canada M2N 3Y5

Printed in Canada

Seasons, rather than clocks and calendars, are what really shape our lives. Minute and second hands and dates on a chart may help us with the petty business of measuring our days and weeks and months, but it is the state of the weather that manipulates our moods and modifies our deeds. Heat, cold, wind, snow and rain rule us, sometimes subtly, sometimes harshly, and while we may often choose to defy them, even then they have had their effect on us; in the end they usually have their way. And, of course, we have to be aware that though the seasons are despots, they are benevolent despots that commonly provide us with the essentials by which we live.

Canada's seasons match its size in splendor and influence. While we may happen to inhabit more than half a continent, it is the half closer to the North Pole than to the Equator, so we are never in doubt about the power of winter and never short in our appreciation of summer. Having learned to endure in a climate of vast extremes, we Canadians make the most of its small mercies: a winter that arrives a week or two late, a summer that comes a few weeks early, a cloudless day in February, a snow cover that is a few centimetres less than the year previous.

Visitors from more temperate countries tend to stand in awe of Canada's climate and to be easily impressed by its extremes. With more snow each winter than those temperate lands may see in a decade, our climate may seem fit only for masochists or supermen to live in, and we are not averse to posing in the latter role. But as the slightest experience will confirm, the often violent and usually humid weather of the tropics imposes an environment far less bearable than our own. It is no mere accident of genetics that the more energetic and prosperous societies lie in latitudes similar to ours.

If our climate were different, we would be a different people. And it could be argued, indeed, that seasonal variations as much as differences of culture account for contrasts in character between, say, British Columbians and Maritimers, or between Northerners and Westerners.

"My country is not a country it's the winter," is how the Quebec poet, Gilles Vigneault, described that key to Canadian character, the dominance of winter as a season. Winter, as the earliest Canadians soon realized, will starve and kill you if you let it. The result is that uniquely dogged pragmatism that enables us to behave as though winter is of little account. Of so little account, indeed, that we have adapted its most fearsome weapon to provide us with a national sport, ice hockey. We have come to terms with winter here, and now love it more than we dread it. And even our slight dread of it has served to intensify our delight in the other seasons. As the following words and pictures may suggest, no season in Canada, not even winter, is empty of joy and warmth and colour.

Pacific Dogwood, floral
emblem of British Columbia.

Spring

Despite the eagerness with which it is welcomed, spring advances very cautiously into Canada. It must oust a very formidable winter that holds on to some parts of the country for as long as six months. So spring takes its time, often disregarding the official date of its arrival.

Advancing from the Pacific, it makes its first foray into southern British Columbia, usually in February, and stakes its claim first with the delicate crocus, then with the ebullient daffodil, and eventually with the Pacific dogwood, that province's emblemic flower. As British Columbians pride themselves on choosing so delectable a homeland, newspapers in the still freezing North and East enviously report these Western blossomings; at Easter florists throughout the country profitably market that evidence that spring is on its way.

But east of the Rockies, the wait tends to be long and agonizing. Winter, having entrenched its hold over so many months, rarely retreats without many counterattacks. The extraordinary Chinook winds that sometimes break through the Rockies from the southwest, flooding Alberta's foothills with a warm foretaste of summer, make the backlash of later snowstorms all the harder to bear. Chinook fever, however illusory, is a delirium more severe than the customary cabin fever suffered by Canadians who get no such reprieve from winter.

Many Canadians, of course, have emulated the Canadian goose and flown south to Florida, Carolina, and the Caribbean for respite. Their incongruous suntans in February and March are an affront to those pallid neighbours and workmates who have dourly soldiered the winter out.

The final stages of winter's rearguard battle are the most frustrating to endure. On city sidewalks, the caked black ice seems even harder than the concrete it so treacherously covers. An April snowfall, clogging suburban driveways, always seems heavier in the snow-shovel than any of the dozen falls that may have preceded it. And in the country, where a heavy winter of snow may guarantee a lush harvest in the fall, farmers are nonetheless impatient for sight of the black earth and the misty green of new growth. Even the mud that will come with the thaw seems preferable to the spine-jolting ruts that cold has etched into unpaved tracks and roads.

But at last winter, however reluctantly, does begin to back off. Ice fishermen, after many official warnings, grudgingly admit that it's time to trundle their huts to shore over the water-slick ice of lakes and rivers. Skiers abandon hope that one last snowfall will restore the surface of the favourite runs. The mountains of salt in highway depots are now reduced to molehills, and the snowploughs in their massive ranks wait in vain for a final emergency call.

The days subtly extend themselves and the sun catches the crystal filagree at the edges of snowbanks. Tendrils of water begin to inch down watersheds, halted by frosty nights, but melting and growing irresistibly as each day's warmth increases. Soon the tinkle of dripping water is drowned by the eager gasp of streams. Ice rattles loose, joins the foaming thud and thunder of river break-up.

Lakes, meanwhile, with more deliberation, undermine and engulf the ice that has held them prisoner.

The plains and hillsides, piebald with drifts, emerge brown and tousled from their months of sleep. Birds breach every dawn more stridently, small animals dart and forage with greater daring. Human Canadians, shedding overcoats and mufflers and toe-rubbers, begin to stand outside and breathe, sipping the cool sunlight as an aperitif of summer. Children, at last free on soggy lawns and lots, mime their lively delight that spring is here.

The Barren Lands of Baffin Island, Northwest Territories, while they do lie beyond the tree line, are far from barren, supporting a wildlife that ranges from the snowy owl to the caribou.

Spring is slow in coming to the Continental Divide in Jasper National Park, Alberta. The peaks of the Rockies are never entirely free of snow and remain a towering reminder to passing travellers and visiting tourists that in a few months winter will again begin its invasion of the high country.

Like the Rockies, Newfoundland's shores are haunted by wintery ghosts. Icebergs, riding south on the Labrador Current from the edge of the northern icefield, often barricade the island's harbours. Adrift in the region's notorious fogs, they are a deadly hazard that local fishermen have learned to live with.

The earliest way of crossing the ice-choked St. Lawrence at Quebec City was by bateau partly rowed and partly hauled across packed icefloes.

Today transport to Levis, across the river, is by ferry bumping its way through the spring ice.

For prairie farmers who recall the dustbowl conditions of the Thirsty Thirties, spring flooding seems always a blessing in disguise. Nevertheless they eye spring as they would an erratic business partner, always liable to do the wrong thing, thawing too suddenly, lapsing into late frosts, galloping hot-headed into a drought. (Legislative Building, Regina, Saskatchewan)

The expanse of Ontario and the effect of the Great Lakes produces strange springtime anomalies. The Niagara fruit belt may swelter under a rehearsal of summer while a hundred miles north the snowbelt still lives up to its name. Farm animals welcome even the freedom to munch frost-browned grass, but it will be months before water-skiers trace white arabesques on the surface of Rice Lake.

Prince Edward Islanders take a certain pride in their isolated exposure to the elements. Like other Maritimers they often see more snow and rain in a year than inlanders have ever dreamed of, but the surrounding salt water melts winter away more quickly, dousing the red soil in preparation for the planting of potatoes.

The woods along Quebec's Gatineau River show off the sylvan fertility that attracted and held the first settlers to this edge of the continent. Winter falls heavily on this region and spring filters life back into the leafless trees as snow and ice disappear. The shimmer of vivid green on the branches is a modest dress rehearsal for the glory that will be perfected by the fall.

For all the range of its power and influence across Canada, Ottawa remains a small city rather than a metropolis. Its citizens, most of them desk-bound through the working day, have a common contrasting enthusiasm for sports and pastimes out of doors, whichever the season. At last free of the heavy winter that the Ottawa Valley invariably dumps on them, they celebrate spring with a festival in a green city park. Parliament and its grey cares is behind them for the moment.

Proud as Halifax may be of its venerable Clock Tower, this seaport and garrison has never paid much attention to man-made time. Its working rhythm has been dictated largely by tide and weather and their effects on shipping. Its busiest months were, and to a degree still are, the months when ice closes the St. Lawrence. So spring is a time for Haligonians to relax a bit in whatever sunshine the Atlantic's moods allow them.

The depth of winter snow on the Prairies is as much a matter of concern for migrating birds as it is for farmers. The sloughs formed by the thaw serve as refreshing stop-overs for these whistling swans on their annual flight from the southern American seaboards to their breeding grounds in Alaska and the Arctic. Their noisy passage is as much a part of prairie spring as the bursting of buds.

The inshore fishermen of Nova Scotia fish as late as they can in the fall and as early as they can in the spring. Their's is less an industry than a way of life, and few lives are more minutely shaped by the seasons. The re-painting and fixing of lobster boats in Neil's Harbour in spring is as much a celebration as an annual chore.

The covered market in Saint John, New Brunswick, is said to be the oldest in the country. And it's probable that during all its springs, with sun limelighting the produce and with heavy winter clothes replaced by something fancier, people have felt more inclined to pause and gossip with old friends.

Manitoba's Red River is a part of the legend of the Prairies, where any water is as revered as a god. But in the wake of a sudden spring thaw, it can be an awe-inspiring god. Even as well-founded a community as Winnipeg must watch with trepidation as the water levels rise. But when you have a river, you just have to learn to live with it. It's like one of the family.

In British Columbia spring
comes both early and late.
Skiers clutch at winter on
Grouse Mountain, while
flowers bloom in Vancouver's
gardens below.

The coming of spring is even more momentous to wildlife than it is to man. With the promise of warm days ahead, the cycle of life begins again for the white-tailed deer.

The short springs of Ontario are relished most as a prelude to months of summer. Rain showers wash the roadways clean of winter salt. Flower-beds and vegetable patches are forked over and planted. Storm-windows are removed and stored in the basement. And at last, when the sun is strong enough to suggest a walk in Toronto's High Park, what better than to take along a folding chair, soak up a little of the warmth and rest a bit. The easy ways of summer need to be practised.

Bareback riding at the rodeo,
High Prairie, Alberta.

Summer

Summer in Canada is the celebration of release. While winter may offer enjoyment and challenge to the athletic and the hardy, every Canadian suffers some sense of confinement when snow envelopes the land and cold slows life down. But as the sun moves higher in the sky, horizons seem to expand and beckon. The earth, drying under its new grass, takes on a resilience that invites a stride and a skip and a jump. Trees that were as stark as scarecrows three months ago are now plump with leaves and generous with shade. Lakes ripple and are bearably warm; rivers invite fishermen and latterday voyageurs.

Space is one of the unique benefits enjoyed by Canadians. A lifetime is not long enough to become familiar with all of the country. And so, when at last summer has opened all the highways and lengthened the days, Canadians love to head off for somewhere new. Less than a day's drive from any city, it is possible to be entirely alone in the wilderness and to experience something of the wonder early pioneers knew as they opened up the land. There are tens of thousands of lakes where a fisherman can fish all day in company only of loons and blackflies. Rivers rarely rippled by canoes. Beaches unmarked by human footsteps.

For the less venturesome, there is the traditional routine of the summer cottage. Often a family inheritance, the cottage is commonly opened in May, occupied fully as soon as school is out, with breadwinners commuting at weekends until their own vacations arrive. Over the halcyon months of July and August, youngsters take on the tones of toast as they cavort with powerboats and waterskis, skim the wind in sailboats, or fool around in canoes. Housewives idle through minimal variations of snacks and salads. Breadwinners lounge and officiate over the sunset ritual of barbecue.

Those without tenure on a summer place pursue the vagrancy of campers and mobile homes, the camaraderie of overnight communities in provincial and national parks, the fun of minor misfortunes and of making do, the surprise of suddenly-discovered beauty, the filing away of bright images for winter remembrance. Canadians in summer are like their squirrels, eagerly storing away kernels of pleasure to sustain them through the long cold months.

Among many young Canadians from cities, summer camp may be their first encounter with the wilderness and their first separation from family. Here lifelong friendships take root and sometimes a nostalgia for the outdoors that lasts as long.

For many other Canadians, of course, farmers and fishermen, construction and other outdoor workers, the seasons are reversed. To make up for the enforced leisure of winter freeze-up, they must work the summer through, and good weather is such a bounty for them that few have the inclination or the time to complain. And besides, they enjoy a certain compensation in being able to take things easier when the rest of Canadians are battling their way to work in the cold.

In summer, whether at leisure or at work, we inhabit the Canada we remember most happily, a country of long days and open roads and wide horizons, of warmth and colour and carefree movement.

Summers are often short in Newfoundland and both wildflowers and people make the most of them. For a few months the sea stops flaunting its boisterous strength, even though it never loses its glacial cold. It's on days like this that Newfoundlanders know for sure why they cherish life on their rugged island. (St. George's Bay, Port Au Port Peninsula)

Quebec City's Winter Carnival may draw thousands to its rigorous revels, but just as many visitors swarm through North America's oldest capital all summer. Few fail to visit the Rue du Trésor, where Quebec artists offer their reflections of the style of New France.

Material success may often seem of more interest to Torontonians than leisure, but as soon as the weather is warm enough they swarm aboard the ferries that will carry them to the string of island parks that separate the harbour from Lake Ontario. There they can picnic or play or swim or sail. Or just lie and contemplate the soaring city in which they take such pride.

For those who love to burn off energy outdoors, British Columbia offers a wealth of opportunity. Kootenay National Park is large enough and remote enough to offer solitary treks through valleys carved by the Ice Age. Winds off a nearby glacier preserve heavy snowdrifts well into the summer.

Some hikers prefer the tide-fretted coastline of British Columbia to the austere mountains. Here in Pacific Rim National Park the trees of the rain forest crowd perilously close to the ocean and every beach is littered with weathered skeletons of driftwood.

Life is still lived simply on Prince Edward Island, and on a scale that befits Canada's smallest province. Those qualities, and modest summer weather, attract many visitors who need relief from the hustle and humidity of inland cities. The strawberries and new potatoes and lobsters that grace the island are additional inducements.

On the Prairies in summer the two centres of attention are the sky and the soil. Early summer normally provides enough rain to get growth going. But, whether you're growing wheat or raising livestock, you need a fair succession of warmth and showers throughout the summer. For all the apprehension with which they are watched, the vastness of the prairie and the vivid arch of its sky are beauties that few of its people could bear to live without.

Athabasca is a name nowadays associated with the great tar-sands project, which is helping appease Canada's energy hunger. But the Athabasca River long precedes that in fame. It has been a highway for explorers, traders and trappers throughout Alberta's settled history, and is still used throughout the warmer months for both commerce and adventurous recreation.

The Atlantic's powerful tides meeting the mighty outflow of the St. Lawrence makes for fine beaches on Prince Edward Island. Another bonus for those visitors drawn to the quiet ways of the island and its fine cuisine.

The citizens of Vancouver regard Stanley Park with both pride and affection. Within easy reach of the city's downtown, it offers space for every kind of outdoor recreation during most of the year. In summer, of course, its beaches are rarely empty. To be a British Columbian is to be sun-tanned and to love cavorting in the warm waters of the Pacific Ocean.

Only in summer can tourists make the boat trip that enables them to photograph and wonder at Percé Rock, off the eastern tip of Quebec's Gaspé Peninsula. Reputedly the landfall of Samuel de Champlain in 1607, it was so named by him because it had been pierced by tidal erosion. 1500 feet long, and rearing 300 feet into the pellucid Atlantic sky, it seems an appropriate gatepost for Canada.

Tourists spending their summer vacation in British Columbia are forever taken aback by the contrasts they encounter. A warm humid rain forest along the coast, towering ranges of mountains perpetually capped by snow, vast powerful rivers, and then, suddenly, in the midst of all this, a desert. The The Great American Desert does reach all the way from Mexico deep into the heart of British Columbia, so parched and hot in summer that it provides sustenance for only a few semi-wild horses.

Clear across the country, under the salty temperamental climate of Newfoundland lies a desert of a quite different kind. Aided by powerful winds, the sand dunes of Gros Morne National Park gradually extend their dominion, engulfing and stifling trees, but providing sanctuary for wayfaring wildfowl, and a glimpse of true wilderness for a few awed visitors every summer.

Ontario's Sibley Provincial Park lies on the southern edge of the Canadian Shield, the vast outcrop of volcanic rock scoured clean by the retreat of the Arctic icecap.

The park, on a rocky promontory reaching into the blue glacial water of Lake Superior, preserves the wilderness that has evolved over 600 million years. Here you can lie and experience the vastness and mystery that enticed the first explorers deeper and deeper into the country.

The teeming wealth of fish around the Grand Banks off Newfoundland has attracted fishing fleets from Europe for hundreds of years. Although competition for this diminishing harvest continues between those and the Canadian and American fleets for most of the year, summer lessens the hardships and dangers. These Portuguese fishermen, stretching their legs on the harbourfront of St. John's are probably as familiar with it as they are with their home port of Lisbon.

Maple leaves, Parry Sound,
Ontario.

Fall

Canadians sip their fall with the appreciative care that connoisseurs give to a vintage wine. A fine reliable summer followed by a long and gradual fall leaves an aftertaste that will be recalled for many years.

Invariably its arrival is anticipated. The delight of crunching into the first butter-dripping cob of fresh corn is usually tempered by a melancholy awareness that fall is only a few weeks away. Labour Day, the first Monday in September, traditionally brings vacations to an end. The seats of school and office desks stand ready to chafe and constrict legs brown and sinewy from trekking and running and swimming. But outside, for only a slightly shorter time each passing day, the tantalizing sun will go on shining. Every moment that can still be spent under its warm benevolence is savoured: backyard suburban patios are heavily populated in early evening, barbecues char their last steaks and hamburgers for disaffected commuters. At weekends, picnics in the park extend the illusion of parole from a working world. The closing up of summer cottages is postponed as long as flesh can ignore the hints of early frost.

Farmers leave summer less reluctantly, since fall is their payday. Until crops are gathered in, there is no end to their anxieties; the eyes that throughout summer scanned the horizon for storm-clouds must now watch for omens of early fall rain or frost. If it has remained unscathed, the grain stands golden and heavy-headed in the fields, willing to surrender to the roaring blitzkreig of harvesters. Macintosh apples are blush-ing furiously, Northern Spies allow a more modest flush, and Russets are uniformed in matt kahki; pears are approaching their jaundiced moment of truth. Tomatoes are vividly threatening their puny withered vines with collapse, eager for the security of cans and pickling jars. Musty grapes are already on their way to the vats of wineries. Rutabagas wait to be waxed, sturdy carrots and plump potatoes to be stored. Pumpkins and squash patiently litter the fields, ready to play their traditional roles in Hallowe'en and Thanksgiving.

Indian summer, fall rearguard of the real thing, makes its last stand under the flamboyant banners of the trees. But inevitably, in November, snap frosts and slashing rainstorms signal the coming of an overwhelming offensive. Raking lawns clear of leaves, oiling and storing garden tools and furniture, and putting up storm windows are obsequies for summer rather than preparations for winter. When we can see the wan sky clear through the bared branches, when we start fine tuning the thermostat in early evening, we know it is time to go find the snow shovel and to wonder if we shouldn't replace lost gloves and leaking snowboots.

Fall, despite the regret its name seems to intimate, usually leaves us with a full barn of remembered pleasure to see us through the winter. It is in fall, when most of Nova Scotia's many visitors have passed, that Cape Breton's Cabot Trail puts on its finest show. The turning colours of the woods, diffused by misty sunlight, imitates impressionistic art, and on still days the North River doubles the visual impact.

Cool fall temperatures yellow
the deciduous trees scattered
amongst the conifers at Split
Peak in Kootenay National
Park in eastern British
Columbia.

Even Prince Edward Island's famous greenness can't outlast the fall. These cattle, near Nail Pond, conditioned perhaps by experience of the island's rambunctious winters, make the best of the grazing while the going is good.

Not a rural game of lawn bowling, but the Ontario pumpkin harvest. Any child who has revelled in the scary frolics of Hallowe'en or any adult who has savoured the seasonal richness of pumpkin pie knows that this is a serious occupation.

Seasons, as balky in their ways as human beings, write the work schedules for farmers. From the moment he plants the seed, the prairie grain farmer can only watch and hope and wait until time is ripe to start the harvester and head out for the fields.

Fall colours in western
Canada are composed of
shades of yellow and lack the
red of the east. This is readily
apparent in the view from
Baldy Mountain, the highest
point in Manitoba.

It is sometimes hard to believe that in a few weeks the trees in Fredericton, New Brunswick will be stark and bare, that the flowerbeds still nourishing a few late flowers will be buried under snow.

And so it is difficult to admit at last that the garden chairs we lounged in, sipping frosty lemonade and chatting during August, must be brought in and stowed away for more than half a year.

Fall has many ways of signal-
ling its slow departure, the
trees, the slowly shrinking
days. And winter too has
means of warning of its im-
minent arrival. Certain
days in late fall, the light takes
on the steely glint of the
winter ahead, a glint and
impersonality that somehow
accords with the architecture
of the University of Calgary.

The trees of Prince Albert National Park, with some help from the fall sunshine, emulate the gold of Saskatchewan's southern wheatfields, now safely harvested.

Cornstalks wither in the gardens of Quebec's Notre Dame du Lac and Lake Temisquata takes on a cloudy chill as fall colour brightens the trees on the surrounding hills.

Some years, in some regions, the impatience of winter cannot be held in check. An opening salvo of snow has dusted the woods near Huntsville, Ontario, enhancing the normal fall spectrum of scarlet, yellow, brown and green. An encouraging omen for skiers, who swarm to the area's several ski runs every weekend of winter and for whom every fall goes on too long.

oronto, by some benign
quirk of geography and cli-
nate, is usually spared both
arly and heavy snowfalls.
Envious neighbours in the
nowbelt to the north attri-
ute many Torontonian flaws
f character to this odd
eprieve, but Torontonians
hemselves take it for granted
s one of the many superior
menities of their city. Boys,
vho'd probably prefer to be
obogganing here in High
Park, console themselves by
oretending it's still high
ummer.

Late in the year the hills of
the Cape Breton Highlands in
Nova Scotia take on a blend of
colours that must have awak-
ened a heartbreaking nostalgia in the first Scottish
settlers here, that of the
Highlands they had been
forced to leave. It is no
wonder that in this adopted
homeland even their de-
scendents try to preserve
many Scottish traditions and
the use of Gaelic.

In the Maritimes as across the land in British Columbia, rain is the prelude to winter. Frost does not come as quickly as other places to strip the fall colours from the woods, but the rain and the storms that are as inevitably a part of fall will soon have just the same effect. On so broad a front winter can never be sure of a general advance, but it is always assured of an eventual victory. (Near Mactaquac, New Brunswick)

Already down the spine of the Rockies, where it maintains garrisons on the peaks the year round, winter has broken through and the landscape here at Sulphur Mountain, Banff National Park, Alberta seems posed for use as a Christmas card. There will be no retreat and the following sky is full of snowy reinforcements. Within a week or two, hikers and mountain-climbers will have been replaced by skiers.

Not far short of where the tree line dwindles and the sub-Arctic taiga begins, the stack of the smelter at Flin-Flon, Manitoba looks like a giant lonesome pine stripped by the wind. The lowering sky of late fall leaves little about weather prospects to the imagination. For deep rock miners it makes little difference.

The jetty at Rice Lake, Ontario where only months ago water-skiers yelled above the growling to-and-fro of power-boats, is empty. The sun looks in occasionally, but its warmth has gone and the people and pleasure with it, and the cottages along the shore are shuttered and asleep. Stealthily, seemingly so fragile at first, ice edges out from the shore, but soon it will impose its iron rule clear across the lake.

Farmhouse, near Elora,
Ontario.

Winter

Since ours is a country of the North, winter is never entirely out of our thoughts no matter what the season. In spring we enjoy relief from it, in summer we exalt in freedom from it, and in the fall we live in anticipation of its coming. Yet when it does come to stake its annual claim over our country, we find that our familiarity with it has bred a certain contempt for its powers.

Most of us are obliged to live almost half our lives out in various degrees of cold weather, so we do not allow it to constrain us very much. Snow and cold and ice are facts of our way of life; they endow us with some of our virtues as a people and provide us with many of our pleasures.

The first fresh fall of snow, however dreaded in anticipation, invariably turns out to be something of a delight. Its arrival from a deadpan sky, hesitant at first, then winding with increasing speed in long white strands, never fails to hypnotize. And awakening to gaze out on a familiar street or landscape, mutely sheeted over with snow for the first time, induces a unique giddy elation. Those first creaking footsteps across new snow offer another sensation worth remembering, even if they take you to the snow shovel you need to clear front steps and driveway. And even then,

although mutual complaints about the chore of snow shovelling are a Canadian tradition, there is a satisfaction in skillfully scooping and hefting furrows of snow from a driveway that no motorized snowblower can provide.

Our secret Canadian love affair with winter is, of course, inherited from childhood. Kids love change and challenge, and winter provided both in plenty: snowballs and snowmen, sidewalk sliding and tobogganing, snowshoeing and skiing, and inevitably our national sport, ice hockey.

And as adults our reaction to winter's assault remains a sportive response to a challenge. We smile condescendingly when news comes of less hardy countries being engulfed and paralyzed by sudden unexpected snowfalls. Even in our most congested cities the inevitable heavy fall rarely slows the rhythm of life for more than half a day. We take pride in carrying on as though nothing untoward had happened, in extricating our cars from snowdrifts, in blithely driving over iced pavements, and in knowing how to get frozen motors running. We know how to dress for winter and and how to maintain summer heat in our homes and workplaces the year round. This disdain for our winter may be a charade, but it works.

Outside the cities, winter is not even considered a challenge. Of necessity it brings much farming and fishing to a temporary halt. But outside workers, after a busy fall and summer feel entitled to slow down. Grain and root-crop growers can gaze with satisfaction on the heaviest fall of snow because it represents future irrigation of their fields. Beef farmers can share in that satisfaction because nowadays they fatten their stock on grain. The innovation of the snowmobile enables them to visit around more easily, to hunt and trap more widely and to ice-fish more comfortably on frozen rivers and lakes. By tradition farmers and fishermen are entitled to grumble about the weather, but they don't complain about the seasons, and certainly not about winter.

For us Canadians, winter is as familiar and as close as a member of the family. Exaggerated in its ways perhaps, sometimes irritating, but with virtues that we can see most clearly. Without our winter we would be a different people, and much less ourselves.

Snow on the gentle undulations of the prairie seems to further expand the staggering immensity of the blue sky. A shrinking congregation has left this church abandoned on a ridge top near Melville, Saskatchewan. It still serves to remind the older folk nearby of those long-past wintery Sunday mornings when, irresistible as a magnet, it drew in horse-drawn cutters and uppity jalopies from miles around.

"My country is not a country
it's the winter . . .
My road is not a road it's the
snow . . ."

Gilles Vigneault's song may
be so popular in Quebec
because Quebeckers have
seen more winters than the
rest of us. They are veterans
of the winter's annual cam-
paigns, and the assaults have
always been heavy. Yet
Quebeckers greet the snow
and the freeze-up like long-
lost friends. There is an air of
celebration about the crowds
that disport themselves on
Montreal's Beaver Lake. Vive
l'hiver!

For all of being spared the
heavy falls of Ontario's snow
belt, Toronto is granted a
respectable share of winter.
And it would take much more
snow than this to slow the
intent pursuit of business that
sets the city's rhythm. Slush-
filled gutters may turn sober
pedestrians into athletes, but
street-cars and subways will
run impeccably to schedule,
and certainly the ticker-tape
on Bay Street will not be
impeded by one split-second.
Torontonians may some-
times feel themselves snowed
under by work but never by
snow.

The Prairie in winter can be awesome in its desolation. It may suffer lighter snowfalls than the East and the Pacific hinterland, but persistent rockbottom temperatures preserve what snow there is and winds drift it over every obstacle. Drivers may not need warning of approaching trains, but they do need to know exactly where the crossing lies buried.

The rolling wooded hills of Manitoba's parkland diminish the scale of the landscape and attract heavier snowfalls. In normal winter weather hardier livestock is left outdoors and seems to thrive better there than when cooped up in barns. Animals need no guidance on the fact that food means survival and these horses are able to cater for their needs no matter how much snow conceals the fodder pile.

The one element of Nova Scotia's climate that is not moderate is its snowfall. Moisture-saturated ocean winds colliding with frigid Northern ones dump lavish snowfalls on the province every year. But Nova Scotians, like Canadians everywhere, just shrug and dig out. And besides, in a community that depends largely on farming and fishing, who needs to go anywhere in weather like that?

Quebeckers so love to fish that winter never deters them. On the Sainte-Anne River at La Pérade this village annually appears on the thick ice. Inside the rented huts, with all the comforts of home and many cases of beer, sportsmen haul up through holes in the ice millions of guileless tommycods every season.

In any season Quebec's Laurentian Hills retain a quality that attracts sight-seers, cameras and artists. Even under heavy snow it remains uniquely pictur-esque. For all their dedication to their sport, these skiers near St. Jovite just have to stop and stare.

Nothing is spared from winter's inflexible discipline. The earth is subdued, trees stand in rigid obedience. Even the mighty flow of New Brunswick's Saint John River is held in check.

Canada's remaining herds of American bison are safely sequestered in wilderness parks, mostly in the North. Thousands of years had conditioned them to survive even the severest winters, but did nothing to protect them from virtual extinction by hunters in the 19th-century. The meat they provided was the first attraction, but understandably their heavy weatherproof pelts were prized by humans less well-conditioned to endure Canada's climate.

Under normal conditions, snow fences can prevent highways and homesteads from being overwhelmed by snow, but sometimes in Ontario's snowbelt even the snow fences are overwhelmed.

Outlined against the snow-fields and like a column of giants, trees march down a valley in Yoho National Park. While the snowfalls of south-eastern British Columbia may delight skiers, the less energetic prefer them in their original form, as mild winds from the Pacific.

Wreathed in cloud, the Dome Glacier in Alberta's Jasper National Park glowers from a high valley like a white-faced dragon. Formed by the weight of continually-replenished snowfields above, the deep compressed river of ice will continue its imperceptible descent as long as the local climate remains unchanged.

eggy's Cove, Nova Scotia, as
w of its annual thousands of
ghtseers ever do see it. The
cal people like the cove no
atter what the weather's
ke, but with a marked bias
wards weather good enough
 fish in.

Another of Canada's legend-
ary sights, the Horseshoe
Falls at Niagara Falls,
Ontario. Understandably,
most visitors, and particularly
those on honeymoon, choose
to come in the warmer
months. But the vast ice-
bridge that forms below the
Falls in winter and the glaze
of frozen mist on every
nearby object are additional
wonders worth beholding.

In a sense the Falls are aptly
symbolic of Canadians themselves - they carry on no
matter what the weather.

Val Clery, born in Ireland, settled in Canada in 1965 and has since established himself as a versatile broadcaster and writer. In both roles he has travelled widely throughout his adopted homeland and has developed a fascination with its rich diversity. He has contributed to most major Canadian magazines and was founding editor of *Books in Canada.* His first book, with Hounslow Press, was the great bestseller *Canada in Colour*, which also featured the photography of Bill Brooks. Other books include *Canada From the Newsstands*, *Doors*, *Windows*, and a children's book, *A Day in the Woods*.

Bill Brooks has been deeply involved with photographing the natural beauty of Canada and with the production of illustrated books since his graduation from the University of Toronto in 1962.

As photo editor for McClelland & Stewart from 1967 to 1972, he was involved in the creation of fine illustrated books. It was during this period, while working on projects extolling the wonders of Canada, that he realized, like most Canadians, just how little he knew about his country.

He set out on a journey of discovery in 1972, with the hope of finding both the real Canada and his place in it. Since then he has produced: *Canada in Colour* (1972), *Ottawa: A Portrait of the Nation's Capital* (1973), *The Mill* (1976), *Wildlife of Canada* (1976), *The Colour of Ontario* (1977), *The Colour of Alberta* (1978). And now, *Seasons of Canada*.